Sara Swan Miller

True Bugs

When Is a Bug *Really* a Bug?

Franklin Watts - A Division of Grolier Publishing
New York • London • Hong Kong • Sydney • Danbury, Connecticut

For Heinz Meng, who taught me the difference

Photographs ©: Alan & Linda Detrick: 7 left; Animals Animals: 5 top right (Patti Murray); Ellis Nature Photography: 1 (Michael Durham), 5 bottom left (Gerry Ellis); Frederick D. Atwood: 43; Photo Researchers: 31 (Tom Branch), 29 (Danny Brass), 25 (Ken Brate), 17 (Scott Camazine), 6 (Ray Coleman), 23 (Stephen Dalton), 7 right (Nuridsany et Pérennou), 13 (Harry Rogers), 5 top left (David M. Schlesser/Nature's Images), 37 (Gregory K. Scott), 42 (Vanessa Vick); S.A. Marshall: 19; The Image Works: 41 (R. Sidney); Visuals Unlimited: 39, 40 (Bill Beatty), 21 (R. Lindholm), 35 (Gary Meslanos), 33 (Glenn Oliver), 15, 27 (Kjell B. Sandved), cover (Leroy Simon), 5 bottom right (Richard Walters).

Illustrations by Jose Gonzales and Steve Savage.

Visit Franklin Watts on the Internet at:
http://publishing.grolier.com

Library of Congress Cataloging-in-Publication Data

Miller, Sara Swan.
True bugs: when is a bug really a bug? / Sara Swan Miller
   p. cm. — (Animals in order)
   Includes bibliographical references and index.
   Summary: An introduction to true bugs, a taxonomic order of insects, that includes descriptions of fourteen species and recommendations for finding, identifying, and observing them.
   ISBN 0-531-11479-1 (lib.bdg.)   0-531-15922-1 (pbk.)
   1. Hemiptera—Juvenile literature. 2. Hemiptera—Classification—Juvenile literature.
[1. Insects.] I. Title. II. Series.
QL521.M58   1998
595.7′54—dc21   97-15720
                                                             CIP
                                                             AC

Contents

Is That *Really* a Bug?

"Where did all these bugs come from?"
"There's a bug in my milk!"
"Look at the pretty bug I found!"

You have probably heard people say things like this. Were they really talking about bugs? Most people think that all insects are bugs. They aren't.

Bugs are actually a special group of insects. Which of the creepy-crawlies you see every day are true bugs? Read on! This is your chance to become a bug expert.

On the next page are four "bugs." But only one is a true bug. Do you know which one?

1. Ladybug

2. Lightningbug

3. Stink bug

4. Spittlebug

Traits of a True Bug

And the answer is . . . number 3! Only a stink bug is a true bug. But how can you tell?

First of all, a true bug has a *beak* with sucking mouthparts. This beak is attached to the front of a true bug's head. The bug holds its beak below its body, between its front legs when it's not devouring a meal.

A bug's front pair of wings is unusual, too. The part of each wing closest to its body is thick and leathery. Toward the tips, these wings are thin and transparent like a fly's wings. The thick part helps protect a second pair of wings underneath. Most true bugs carry their wings crossed over their backs. They overlap to make an "X." A few true bugs have no wings at all.

Many true bugs are shaped like a shield. They have broad shoulders and a narrow tail.

Spined stink bug attacking a caterpillar

6

When young true bugs hatch from their eggs, they look just like their parents, except they are smaller and have no wings. As they grow, true bugs shed their old skinlike outer layer. This layer, which is called an *exoskeleton*, is replaced by a larger one. A bug's wings get bigger each time it sheds.

Many true bugs are plant-eaters. They suck plant juices, and some harm farmers' crops. Some true bugs are meat-eaters. They suck body fluids from other insects or blood from *mammals*.

Some bugs are brightly colored. These colors warn birds that the bugs taste bad or have a bad smell. Other bugs blend well with their surroundings, so it is difficult for their enemies to spot them.

The Order of Living Things

A tiger has more in common with a house cat than with a daisy. A scorpion is more like a butterfly than a jellyfish. Scientists arrange living things into groups based on how they look and how they act. A tiger and a house cat belong to the same group, but a daisy belongs to a different group.

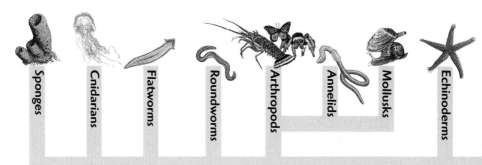

Sponges · Cnidarians · Flatworms · Roundworms · Arthropods · Annelids · Mollusks · Echinoderms

Animals

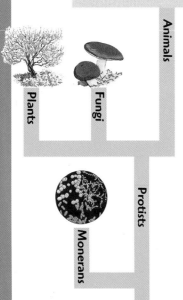

Plants · Fungi · Protists · Monerans

All living things can be placed in one of five groups called *kingdoms:* the plant kingdom, the animal kingdom, the *fungus* kingdom, the moneran kingdom, or the protist kingdom. You can probably name many of the creatures in the plant and animal kingdoms. The fungus kingdom includes mushrooms, yeasts, and molds. The moneran and protist kingdoms contain thousands of living things that are too small to see without a microscope.

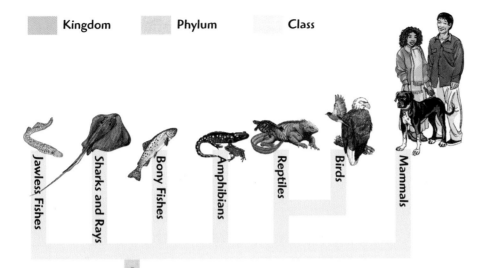

Kingdom   **Phylum**   **Class**

Jawless Fishes

Sharks and Rays

Bony Fishes

Amphibians

Reptiles

Birds

Mammals

Chordates

Because there are millions and millions of living things on Earth, some of the members of one kingdom may not seem all that similar. The animal kingdom includes creatures as different as tarantulas and trout, jellyfish and jaguars, salamanders and sparrows, elephants and earthworms.

To show that an elephant is more like a jaguar than an earthworm, scientists further separate the creatures in each kingdom into more specific groups. The animal kingdom can be divided into nine *phyla*. Humans belong to the chordate phylum. All chordates have a backbone.

Each phylum can be subdivided into many *classes*. Humans, mice, and elephants all belong to the mammal class. Each class can be further divided into *orders*; orders into *families*, families into *genera*, and genera into *species*. All of the members of a species are very similar.

9

How True Bugs Fit In

You can probably guess that true bugs belong to the animal kingdom. They have much more in common with spiders and snakes than with maple trees and morning glories.

True bugs belong to the arthropod phylum. All arthropods have a tough outer skin. Can you guess what other living things might be arthropods? Examples include spiders, scorpions, mites, ticks, millipedes, and centipedes. Many arthropods live in the ocean. Lobsters, crabs, and shrimps are all arthropods.

The arthropod phylum can be divided into a number of classes. True bugs belong to the insect class. Butterflies, ants, flies, and beetles are also insects.

There are thirty different orders of insects. The true bugs make up one of these orders. True bugs can be divided into a number of different families and genera. There are more than 38,000 different species of true bugs.

This book will introduce you to a few of the species that you are most likely to see. As you will soon discover, they live in many different *habitats*—fields, gardens, woods, ponds, and streams. Some probably live in your home—maybe even in your bed!

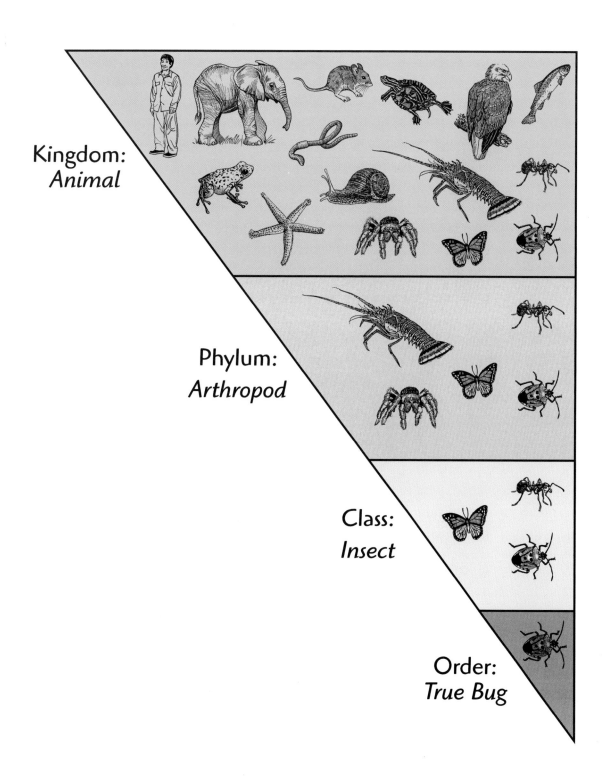

Kingdom: *Animal*

Phylum: *Arthropod*

Class: *Insect*

Order: *True Bug*

11

Seed Bugs

FAMILY: Lygaeidae
COMMON EXAMPLE: Small milkweed bug
GENUS AND SPECIES: *Lygaeus kalmii*
SIZE: 1/8 to 1/2 inch (3 to 13 mm)

The bright-red and black milkweed bug hangs from a leaf on a *milkweed* plant. It looks like a jewel glistening in the sun. This bug is not trying to be beautiful. Its bright colors protect it from its enemies. It's like carrying a big sign that says:

**STOP!
Don't Eat Me!
I Taste Bad!**

The milkweed bug spends its time sucking on the bitter juices of milkweeds. Remember the saying, "You are what you eat"? The milkweed bug tastes as bad as the plant it feeds on. If a bird tries to eat one, it spits the bug right out. The bird will remember to leave those red and black bugs alone!

Many other insects and animals have bright colors that warn enemies to stay away. Can you think of some?

Stink Bugs

FAMILY: Pentatomidae
COMMON EXAMPLE: Harlequin bug
GENUS AND SPECIES: *Murgantia histrionica*
SIZE: 3/8 inch (9.5 mm)

Stink bugs smell bad and taste worse! They leave a stinky, sticky goo wherever they go. Have you ever eaten a bad-tasting piece of fruit? If the fruit didn't look rotten, you were probably tasting stink bug juice.

Believe it or not, some people actually like the taste of stink bugs. People in Mexico, Africa, and India eat them as a special treat.

Some stink bugs are brightly colored. The harlequin bug is brilliant orange, red, yellow, and black. Like the small milkweed bug, its colors say, "Keep away!"

Other stink bugs are the same color as the plants they eat or live on. Because some birds don't mind the smell and taste of stink bugs, the bugs' *camouflage* helps them hide from enemies.

If you look on the underside of cabbage leaves, you may find two neat rows of tiny white raised dots. These are the eggs of a harlequin bug. The female bug almost always lays eggs in two groups of twelve. How did the harlequin bug learn to count?

Ambush Bugs

FAMILY: Reduviidae
COMMON EXAMPLE: Ambush bug
GENUS AND SPECIES: *Phymata fasciata*
SIZE: 3/8 to 1/2 inch (9.5 to 13 mm)

The ambush bugs that live in North America are small, sneaky, and fierce. If you look carefully, you may find one hiding in a goldenrod flower. The bug's yellow-and-brown body matches the colors of its hiding place.

The ambush bug stays perfectly still as it waits for another insect to land. Then it pounces on its victim. It can capture and kill insects twice its size, even bumblebees.

The instant an unsuspecting bee lands, the ambush bug attacks. The bug grabs the bee with its powerful front legs. The bee struggles wildly, but it cannot escape the strong, toothed forelegs clamped around it. The ambush bug then pierces the bee with its sharp beak and sucks the bee's juices, leaving just a dry shell.

An ambush bug might not look like a true bug at first glance. It is not shield-shaped like most bugs—its body is wider at the tail than at the shoulders. It looks as though it has a little skirt sticking out around its knees.

But if you could stretch out its front wings, you would see that they are thick and leathery close to its body and thin near the tip. Don't try it, though! It might think you are another tasty insect!

Damsel Bugs

FAMILY: Nabidae
COMMON EXAMPLE: Gray damsel bug
GENUS AND SPECIES: *Nabis americoferus*
SIZE: 3/8 inch (9.5 mm)

You may have a hard time seeing a gray damsel bug. Its grayish-brown or yellowish body blends with the plants it lurks on. Other insects have a hard time seeing it, too.

When an unsuspecting insect wanders past the damsel bug's hiding place, the bug dashes out and thrusts its sharp beak deep into the body of its victim. In no time at all, it sucks out its *prey's* juices.

Farmers like gray damsel bugs because they feed on many pests that eat crops. They especially like aphids, leafhoppers, plant bugs, and corn ear worms.

In June, a female damsel bug lays about sixty eggs inside the stem of a plant. Six days later the young hatch and start hunting for food. In less than a month, the young grow into adults and start their own families.

Assassin Bugs

FAMILY: Reduviidae

COMMON EXAMPLE: Spined assassin bug

GENUS AND SPECIES: *Sinea diadema*

SIZE: 1/2 to 5/8 inches (13 to 16 mm)

Assassin bugs have long, narrow heads and long, thin necks. Their foreheads are slender, too. They look much too weak to capture prey. But don't let their looks fool you. They will devour just about any insect that comes near. That's why gardeners and farmers like having them around.

Fall is a good time to look for the spined assassin bug in a meadow. You may find one lurking in the flowers of goldenrods, asters, or other plants in the daisy family.

The moment an unsuspecting fly lands on a flower, the spiny bug pounces. The fly struggles wildly to escape, but the fierce assassin bug plunges its beak into the victim's back. The fly is doomed.

Inside the assassin bug's head are two pumps. One of them shoots venom into the fly and turns the its insides to soup. Before the assassin bug sucks up the soup, it uses the second pump to release a second fluid that washes the venom out the bug's beak.

Bed Bugs
FAMILY: Cimicidae
COMMON EXAMPLE: Bed bug
GENUS AND SPECIES: *Cimex lectularius*
SIZE: 1/8 to 1/4 inch (3 to 6 mm)

Nobody loves a bed bug, but it doesn't care. Once it gets into your house, this tiny bug will want to stay with you forever.

During the day, bed bugs hide under mattresses, behind loose wallpaper, in small cracks, and behind baseboards. As soon as the lights go out, bed bugs race out and start biting. Their bite is painful and itchy. But if their sleeping victim wakes up and turns on the light, the bed bugs vanish!

Bed bugs are so small—and so good at hiding—that it is difficult to get rid of them. Sprays may work at first, but if they do not kill the eggs, the bugs will be back. People sometimes try moving away for a while, hoping the bed bugs will die of starvation. But a bed bug can live for a whole year without eating!

You can tell there are bed bugs in a house even before they bite you. They leave a stinky oil behind them wherever they go. That unpleasant smell is a dead giveaway that bed bugs are lurking in their secret places, waiting for "lights-out"!

Flat Bugs
FAMILY: Aradidae
COMMON EXAMPLE: Flat bug
GENUS AND SPECIES: *Aradus quadrilineatus*
SIZE: 3/8 inch (9.5 mm)

Flat bugs are oval, dark, and, of course, flat. It looks as if someone has stepped on them. They have to be flat to fit into their favorite hiding places. You might find them in small cracks or just under the bark of old, decaying trees. But you might easily miss them. They look more like small pieces of bark than like any of the bugs you have met so far.

Most flat bugs are dull-brown or black, but some have reddish markings. At first, you might mistake the reddish ones for bed bugs. But don't worry—flat bugs won't bite you. They're too busy sucking on rotting wood and the fungi that grow on decaying trees.

Flat bugs are very common in wooded areas of North America. But they are so small and so well-hidden that even scientsits don't know very much about them. Look for flat bugs under bark and watch what they do. Maybe you'll find out something that scientists don't know.

Lace Bugs

FAMILY: Tingidae
COMMON EXAMPLE: Sycamore lace bug
GENUS AND SPECIES: *Corythucha ciliata*
SIZE: 1/8 inch (3 mm)

Lace bugs look like little pieces of lace. But they are so tiny that you need a microscope to see how beautiful they are. You may find clusters of them on the undersides of leaves. They suck away at the leaf juices until the leaves are spotted and brown. As you might guess, sycamore lace bugs like sycamore trees best. Sometimes, thousands of them cluster on a grove of *sycamore* trees. Even thousands of these bugs cannot do much damage to the trees, though. When they have eaten their fill, the trees are still leafy—just not quite as green.

Female lace bugs lay their eggs upright in the tissues of leaves and cover them with a sticky, brown film that hardens into small cones on the underside of the leaves. The young are safe in these hard little tepees until they're ready to hatch. When they do, they leave sticky trails on the underside of the leaves.

If you look at the undersides of sycamore leaves or oak leaves with a microscope or hand lens, you may find 100 or more lace-bug babies of different sizes clustered around the adults on a single leaf. If the lace bugs have gone, you may see their tiny cast-off exoskeletons sticking to the leaves.

Scentless Plant Bugs

FAMILY: Rhopalidae
COMMON EXAMPLE: Box elder bug
GENUS AND SPECIES: *Leptocoris trivittatus*
SIZE: 3/8 inch (9.5 mm)

If you look at a *box elder* tree in midsummer, you may see hundreds of box elder bugs on the trunk—from the ground all the way up to the highest branches. The red markings on their black bodies make them easy to spot. You'll see all sizes, from newly hatched young to fully-grown adults. But no matter how many box elder bugs feed on one tree, they don't do much damage.

By fall, most of the young have grown into adults. The bugs migrate in masses and cluster on fences or on the sunny side of houses. Box elder bugs often find their way into houses and snuggle up in a protected place for the winter. Others *hibernate* in cracks in fences or stone walls.

When the buds of the box elder trees begin to open in the spring, the box elder bugs fly out of their winter homes to feed on the leaves and lay their eggs. The females usually lay their eggs under the tree bark or right on the leaves.

You might also spot box elder bugs on fruit trees. They often leave the fruit looking scarred and oddly shaped, but who can really blame them for craving a juicy peach?

Backswimmers

FAMILY: Notonectidae
COMMON EXAMPLE: Backswimmer
GENUS AND SPECIES: *Notonecta undulata*
SIZE: 1/2 inch (13 mm)

The backswimmer really does swim around on its back, which is shaped like the hull of a rowboat. Its two long, fringed back legs work like oars. The bug's coloring helps protect it from enemies. Fish swimming along underneath don't notice it, because its back is light-colored like the sky. Birds flying overhead don't notice it either because its belly is dark, like the pond below.

Before a backswimmer makes a dive, it traps air between rows of hair growing inside grooves on its belly. How does the trapped air get to the bug's nose? It doesn't. Like other insects, the backswimmer doesn't breathe through a nose. Its "nostrils" are little tubes in its belly, called *spiracles*.

Backswimmers are lighter than water, so they have to work hard to stay underwater after they dive. When they get tired of rowing to stay under, they may cling tightly to underwater weeds. When a backswimmer has used up its air supply, it swims up to the surface and traps more air before making another dive.

The backswimmer is a fierce hunter. It can capture an insect, or even a small fish, with its clawed front legs. The bug clasps its prey, sticks in its beak, and sucks its victim dry.

31

Water Boatmen

FAMILY: Corixidae
COMMON EXAMPLE: Water boatman
GENUS AND SPECIES: *Hesperocorixa laevigata*
SIZE: 1/4 to 1/2 inch (6 to 13 mm)

The water boatman looks a lot like the backswimmer. It's about the same size, and it rows about with its long back legs. But it swims right-side-up.

The water boatman carries its air supply under its wings and all around its body. It looks as though it is covered with a silver envelope. It is an even better *scuba* diver than the backswimmer.

In clear water, a waterboatman can breathe the same supply of air over and over again. In stagnant water, the bug needs to come to the surface for air more often.

Unlike most bugs, the water boatman has a soft beak. It is not much good for piercing plants or animals, so the water boatman wanders around the bottom of ponds scooping up ooze with its spoon-shaped front legs. The water boatman sucks on this slimy ooze, which contains algae and tiny animals.

Like the backswimmer, the water boatman can leap out of the water and fly off. Adult water boatmen often fly toward lights. If you live near a pond, you may see them bumbling around your porch light at night.

Water Scorpions
FAMILY: Nepidae
COMMON EXAMPLE: Water scorpion
GENUS AND SPECIES: *Ranatra fusca*
SIZE: 1 1/2 inch (38 mm)

If you have ever seen an insect known as a *walkingstick*, you have some idea of what a water scorpion looks like. It wanders oh-so-slo-o-owly around the bottom of ponds. Fish, and other insects that might want to eat it, usually ignore the water scorpion because they think it's just a little stick moving with the current.

But when the water scorpion spots a victim, the "stick" strikes! Its front legs, which look like two jackknives, snap shut on its insect prey. It pierces its victim's skin and sucks out its juices.

You may see a water scorpion climbing backward up an underwater stem. When it finds just the right spot, it holds on to the stem and lifts its tail end above the surface of the pond. It is taking in air through its snorkel-like tail.

The water scorpion is not much of a swimmer. Its stick-like legs are too thin for this bug to move quickly through the water. But this bug can fly well, if it has to. If the pond it is living in dries up, it can fly for miles until it finds a new home. Imagine seeing a flying stick!

Giant Water Bugs

FAMILY: Belostomatidae
COMMON EXAMPLE: Giant water bug
GENUS AND SPECIES: *Lethocerus americanus*
SIZE: 2 inches (5 cm)

You may find a giant water bug resting on the pond surface, head down. Like the water scorpion, it sticks its snorkel-like tail above the surface to breathe.

The giant water bug is large and very fierce. Its favorite foods include insects, tadpoles, salamanders, and even fish and frogs. A 3-inch (7-cm)-long fish is not too big for a giant water bug to tackle.

It grabs its victim with its large, folding front legs, which snap shut like an animal trap. The prey may put up a good fight, but it won't escape. The giant water bug holds its prey tight and pierces it with a strong, sharp beak. With its sucking mouthparts, the bug slurps up its victim's body juices, leaving only a dried-up carcass.

And watch out! This giant bug can give you a giant, painful bite!

The female has a strange way of protecting her eggs. She sneaks up on a male resting at the surface and grabs him. Then she wraps her legs around him and spreads glue all over his back. She lays 100 or more eggs in the glue. No one dares to try eating the eggs as long as there's a fierce giant water bug guarding them.

Water Striders

FAMILY: Gerridae
COMMON EXAMPLE: Water strider
GENUS AND SPECIES: *Gerris remigis*
SIZE: 3/4 inch (19 mm)

Imagine what it would be like to walk on water! The water strider does it all day long.

It doesn't sink because its long thin legs are water-repellent. The bug stretches them out wide, with just the tips touching the water, so its weight is spread out over a larger area. The water strider is just light enough to be able to skate across the water's surface.

When the water strider is still, the tips of its legs make little dimples in the surface film. The shadow it casts on the bottom of the stream looks like a piece of popcorn.

What happens when a water strider is splashed? Some types of water striders can swim underwater and return to the surface. Others cannot swim. If they are forced underwater, they will drown. You may be wondering what the water strider does when it rains. Many scientists have wondered the same thing, but they have not been able to find an answer. Maybe you'll be the one to discover the water strider's secret.

This bug eats small insects that fall into the water. When the insect struggles to stay afloat, it makes tiny waves that radiate in all directions. The water strider feels these vibrations with its feet, zips across the water, and pounces on its victim.

Water striders are fast, nervous bugs, so it is very hard to catch them, even with a net. If you do catch one, look at it closely. You will notice that water striders don't look like most other true bugs. Their bodies are long and slim, and some have no wings at all. They do have tiny beaks with sucking mouthparts, though. If you look very closely with a hand lens, you can see the water strider's beak tucked under its head.

Looking for Bugs in Fields, Gardens, and Woods

Would you like to become a bug expert? You don't need a lot of fancy equipment.

You don't even need a lot of outdoor space. It's nice to have a big field or woodland to explore, but you can also look for true bugs in a garden, in your backyard, or in a schoolyard. If you live in a city, you can find plenty of true bugs in your local park. There are bugs everywhere.

The best way to find bugs in a field is to get down on your hands and knees with a hand lens. Gently part the grasses and other plants to find bugs down low. Look closely at the leaves and stems.

In tall grass, a sweep net makes it easier to find bugs. Swoosh it back and forth as you walk. Then look inside to see what you collected. Gently put the insects into a jar, so you can examine them more closely.

Useful Tools

A sweep net

Some small, clear plastic jars with lids

A plastic hand lens

A journal to keep track of the bugs you find

An insect field guide

When you have figured out which insects are true bugs, let the rest go. Don't keep the true bugs in the jar too long, either. They may starve or suffocate.

In the woods, look carefully under the bark of trees and on the undersides of leaves. Look closely at plants growing near the ground too. Gently move rocks and sticks to see if there are bugs underneath.

When you find an insect, watch it for a while. Is it a true bug? Where is it going? What is it eating? After you figure out what it's doing in its natural setting, place it in a jar and look at it more closely with a hand lens.

Draw a picture of each bug in your journal. Describe how it moves, what it eats, when and where you found it, and any other information you think is interesting. When you're done, put the bugs back where you found them.

Looking for Bugs in Ponds and Streams

You'll be surprised how many bugs you can find in ponds and streams. All of them have had special problems to solve. How do they get oxygen to breathe when they're underwater? How do they manage to swim around to find their food? Over millions of years, each kind of water bug has found its own ways to adapt.

You can find bugs in every part of a pond—from the surface right down into the muddy bottom. Bugs live in streams, too, especially in the pools with less current.

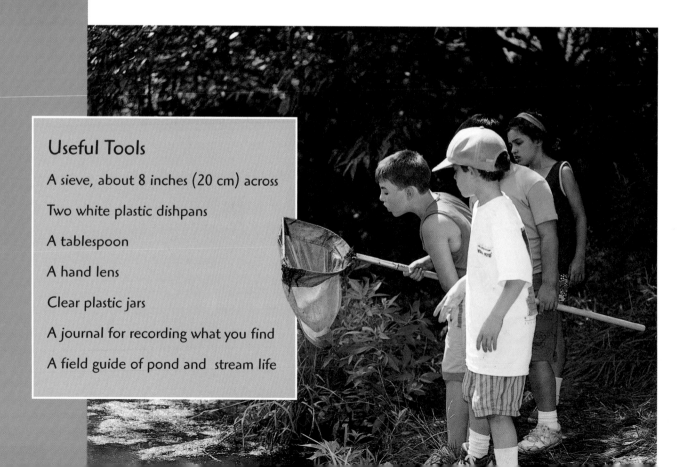

Useful Tools

A sieve, about 8 inches (20 cm) across

Two white plastic dishpans

A tablespoon

A hand lens

Clear plastic jars

A journal for recording what you find

A field guide of pond and stream life

Before you collect any bugs, fill one dishpan half-full with clear pond water. Next, use your sieve to scoop up some watery mud from the pond bottom. Put the mud in the other dishpan. Gently search through the mud in the second dishpan with the tablespoon. When you find an insect, use the spoon to put it in the dishpan with clear water. Now you can watch it easily. Is it a true bug or some other kind of insect? Notice how it moves. Float a leaf on the water and see if the insect wants to hide in the shadow.

If you want to get a closer look, put the insect into a jar with some pond water and look at it with a hand lens. Look for the creature's mouthparts, wings, and eyes. Can you figure out how it breathes?

Once you have placed a few insects in the dishpan of clear water,

watch closely. Do some of them eat others? You can find out more about them from your field guide. You can also use your sieve to scoop bugs from the surface of the water. Add them to the dishpan of clear water and watch what they do.

Note everything you see in your journal. Draw pictures of the bugs you collect and record when and where you found each one.

When you're all done observing the true bugs, lower each dishpan until it is just above the water's surface and gently pour the water back into the pond. The bugs will slip back into their watery world.

Words to Know

beak—the long sucking mouthparts of a true bug.

box elder—a kind of maple tree, usually found near water.

camouflage—coloring and markings that allow an animal to blend in with its surroundings.

class—a group of creatures within a phylum that share certain characterisitics.

family—a group of creatures within a class that share certain characteristics.

fungus (plural fungi)—one of the five kingdoms of living things. Fungi obtain nutrients from decaying plant and animal matter.

exoskeleton—the tough, skinlike covering of insects and some other animals.

genus (plural genera)—a group of creatures within a family that share certain characteristics.

habitat—the environment where a plant or animal lives and grows.

hibernate—to spend the winter in a resting state, with a slowed heart rate and breathing.

kingdom—one of the five divisions into which all living things are placed: the animal kngdom, the plant kingdom, the fungus kingdom, the moneran kingdom, and the protist kingdom.

mammal—an animal that has a backbone and feeds its young with mother's milk.

milkweed—a wildflower with umbrella-like clusters of pinkish flowers. It bears long, pointed seed pods. The seeds have fluff attached to them and are carried by the wind.

order—a group of creatures within a class that share certain characteristics.

phylum (plural phyla)—a group of creatures within a kingdom that share certain characteristics.

prey—an animal hunted by another animal.

scuba (self-contained underwater breathing apparatus)—diving equipment that allows divers to carry their own air supply. Scuba gear was invented by Jacques Cousteau.

species—a group of creatures within a genus that share certain characteristics. Members of a species can mate and produce young.

spiracles—breathing holes, usually on the abdomen, that allow insects to breathe.

sycamore—a deciduous tree with mottled bark that flakes off in jigsawlike pieces. Its leaves are toothed, and it bears brown fruit-balls on long stalks.

walkingstick—an insect that looks like a stick. It belongs to the order Orthoptera and is related to grasshoppers.

Learning More

Books

Cottam, Clarence. *Insects: A Golden Guide*. Racine, WI: Western
  Publishing Co., 1987.

Ganeri, Anita. *Insects*. New York: Franklin Watts, 1993.

Johnson, Sylvia A. *Water Insects*. Minneapolis: Lerner Publications,
  1989.

Leahy, Christopher. *Peterson's First Guide to Insects*. Boston:
  Houghton Mifflin, 1987.

Mound, Laurence. *Amazing Insects*. New York: Knopf, 1993.

CD-ROM

Bug Adventure: An Insect Adventure. Knowledge Adventure, 1995.

Web Sites

The Bug Club Page has a list of insect experts that you can contact
by e-mail. The club also organizes local field trips and publishes a
newsletter six times a year.
http://www.ex.ac.uk/bugclub

The Young Entemologist's Society Page runs a program called
"Bugs-On-Wheels." You may be able to arrange for a bug expert to
visit your school and show your classmates some really cool bugs.
http://insects.ummz.lsa.umich.edu/yes/yes.html

Index

About the Author

Sara Swan Miller has enjoyed working with children all her life, first as a Montessori nursery school teacher, and later as an outdoor environmental educator at the Mohonk Preserve in New Paltz, New York. As the director of the Preserve school program, she has led hundreds of children on field trips and taught them the importance of appreciating and respecting the natural world, especially its less lovable "creepy crawlies."

She has written a number of children's books including *Three Stories You Can Read to Your Dog*; *Three Stories You Can Read to Your Cat*; *What's in the Woods: An Outdoor Activity Book*; *Oh, Cats of Camp Rabbitbone!*; *Piggy in the Parlor and Other Tales*; *Better Than TV*; and *Will You Sting Me? Will You Bite Me? The Truth about Some Scary-Looking Insects*.